I0469306

The U.S.-Colombia Free Trade Agreement:
Background and Issues

M. Angeles Villarreal

Specialist in International Trade and Finance

April 27, 2012

Congressional Research Service

7-5700

www.crs.gov

RL34470

CRS Report for Congress

Summary

The U.S.-Colombia Free Trade Agreement, or U.S. Colombia Trade Promotion Agreement, as it is officially called, is a comprehensive free trade agreement (FTA) between the United States and Colombia, which will eventually eliminate tariffs and other barriers in bilateral trade in goods and services. The agreement will enter into force on May 15, 2012. On October 3, 2011, President Barack Obama submitted draft legislation (H.R. 3078/S. 1641) to both houses of Congress to implement the FTA. On October 12, 2011, the House passed H.R. 3078 (262-167) and sent it to the Senate. The Senate passed the implementing legislation (66-33) on the same day. The agreement was signed by both countries almost five years earlier, on November 22, 2006. The Colombian Congress approved it in June 2007 and again in October 2007, after it was modified to include new provisions agreed to in the May 10, 2007 bipartisan understanding between congressional leadership and President George W. Bush. Upon entry into force, the agreement will immediately eliminate duties on 80% of U.S. exports of consumer and industrial products to Colombia. Most remaining tariffs will be eliminated within 10 years of implementation.

The congressional debate surrounding the CFTA mostly centered on violence, labor, and human rights issues in Colombia. Numerous Members of Congress opposed passage of the agreement because of concerns about alleged violence against union members in Colombia, inadequate efforts to bring perpetrators to justice, and weak protection of worker rights. However, other Members of Congress supported the CFTA and took issue with these charges, stating that Colombia had made great progress over the last ten years to curb violence and enhance security. They also argued that U.S. exporters were losing market share of the Colombian market and that the agreement would open the Colombian market for U.S. goods and services. For Colombia, an FTA with the United States is part of its overall economic development strategy.

To address the concerns related to labor rights and violence in Colombia, the United States and Colombia agreed upon an "Action Plan Related to Labor Rights" that includes specific and concrete steps, with specific timelines, most of which took place in 2011. It contains numerous commitments by the Colombian government to protect union members, end impunity, and improve worker rights. The Colombian government submitted documents to the United States in time to meet various target dates listed in the Action Plan. The USTR reviewed the documents and determined that Colombia had met its major commitments.

The U.S. business community generally supports the FTA with Colombia because it sees it as an opportunity to increase U.S. exports to Colombia. U.S. exporters urged U.S. policymakers to move forward with the agreement, arguing that the United States was losing market share of the Colombian market, especially in agriculture, as Colombia entered into FTAs with other countries. Colombia's FTA with Canada, which was implemented on August 15, 2011, was of particular concern for U.S. agricultural producers.

The United States is Colombia's leading trade partner. Colombia accounts for a very small percentage of U.S. trade (1.0% in 2011), ranking 22nd among U.S. export markets and 23rd as a supplier of U.S. imports. Economic studies on the impact of a U.S.-Colombia free trade agreement (FTA) have found that, upon full implementation of an agreement, the impact on the United States would be positive but very small due to the small size of the Colombian economy when compared to that of the United States (about 2.2%).

Contents

Figures

Tables

Contacts

Introduction

The U.S.-Colombia Free Trade Agreement, or U.S. Colombia Trade Promotion Agreement, as it is officially called, is a comprehensive free trade agreement (FTA) between the United States and Colombia, which will eventually eliminate tariffs and other barriers in bilateral trade in goods and services. On April 15, 2012, at the Summit of the Americas in Cartagena Colombia, President Barack Obama announced that the agreement would enter into force on May 15, 2012, sooner than many observers expected. The announcement came after completion of several months of work by both governments to review each other's laws and regulations related to the implementation of the FTA, as well as to Colombia's efforts to fulfill its set of commitments under the Action Plan Related to Labor Rights.[1] On October 3, 2011, President Barack Obama submitted draft legislation (H.R. 3078/S. 1641) to both houses of Congress to implement the U.S.-Colombia Trade Promotion Agreement. On October 12, 2011, the House passed H.R. 3078 (262-167) and sent it to the Senate. The Senate passed the legislation (66-33) on the same day. The President signed the legislation on October 21, 2011 (P.L. 112-42).

The CFTA negotiations grew out of a regional effort in 2004 to produce a U.S.-Andean free trade agreement between the United States and the Andean countries of Colombia, Peru, and Ecuador. After numerous rounds of talks, however, negotiators failed to reach an agreement, and Colombia continued negotiations with the United States for a bilateral free trade agreement (FTA). On February 27, 2006, the United States and Colombia concluded the U.S.-Colombia FTA, and finalized the text of the agreement on July 8, 2006. On August 24, 2006, President Bush notified Congress of his intention to sign the U.S.-Colombia FTA. The two countries signed the agreement on November 22, 2006. The Colombian Congress approved the agreement in June 2007 and again in October 2007, after the agreement was modified to include new labor and environmental provisions.

Rationale for the Agreement

Since the 1990s, the countries of Latin America and the Caribbean have been a focus of U.S. trade policy as demonstrated by the passage of the North American Free Trade Agreement (NAFTA), the U.S.-Chile Free Trade Agreement, the Dominican Republic-Central America Free Trade Agreement (CAFTA-DR), and the U.S.-Peru Trade Promotion Agreement. Since 2004, U.S. trade policy in the Western Hemisphere has been focused on completing trade negotiations with Colombia, Peru, and Panama and on gaining passage of these free trade agreements by the U.S. Congress. The U.S.-Peru FTA was approved by Congress and signed into law in December 2007 (P.L. 110-138).[2] The U.S.-Panama FTA was approved by Congress shortly after the CFTA on October 12, 2011 and signed into law on October 21, 2011 (P.L. 112-43).

A free trade agreement with Colombia will increase market access for U.S. goods and services in the Colombian market, which is currently limited under the present trade arrangement with Colombia. Under the Andean Trade Preference Act (ATPA), the United States extends unilateral

---

[1] Office of the United States Trade Representative (USTR), *United States, Colombia Set Date for Entry into Force of U.S.-Colombia Trade Agreement,* available at http://www.ustr.gov.

[2] For more information, see CRS Report RL34108, *U.S.-Peru Economic Relations and the U.S.-Peru Trade Promotion Agreement,* by M. Angeles Villarreal.

preferential duty treatment to select Colombian goods entering the United States. It is part of a broader U.S. initiative with Latin America to address the illegal drug issue (see section on ATPA later in this report). About 90% of U.S. imports from Colombia enter the United States duty-free under ATPA, under other U.S. trade preferences, or through normal trade relations.

The major expectation among proponents of the free trade agreement with Colombia, as with other trade agreements, is that it will provide economic benefits for both the United States and Colombia as the level of trade increases between the two countries. Another expectation among proponents is that it will improve investor confidence and increase foreign direct investment in Colombia, which may bring more economic stability to the country. For Colombia, a free trade agreement with the United States is part of the country's overall development strategy and efforts to promote economic growth and stability.

Colombian Tariffs on Goods from the United States

The U.S. average tariff on Colombian goods is 3%, while Colombia's average tariff on U.S. goods is 12.5%. In 2010, about 90% of U.S. imports from Colombia came into the country duty-free under trade preference programs or through normal trade relations. Most of Colombia's duties have been consolidated into three tariff levels: 0% to 5% on capital goods, industrial goods, and raw materials not produced in Colombia; 10% on manufactured goods, with some exceptions; and 15% to 20% on consumer and "sensitive" goods. Exceptions include: automobiles, which are subject to a 35% duty; beef and rice, which are subject to an 80% duty; and milk and cream, which were subject to a 98% duty through August 11, 2010.[3]

Table 1 provides a summary of Colombian tariffs on goods coming from the United States. Other agricultural products fall under the Andean Price Band System (APBS). The APBS protects domestic industry in Colombia, and other Andean countries, with a variable levy by increasing tariffs when world prices fall, and lowering tariffs when world prices rise.[4] The APBS includes 14 product groups and covers more than 150 tariff lines. This system can result in duties exceeding 100%, depending on world commodity prices, for certain U.S. exports to Colombia, including corn, wheat, rice, soybeans, pork, poultry parts, cheeses, and powdered milk.[5]

---

[3] Office of the United States Trade Representative (USTR), *2010 National Trade Estimate Report on Foreign Trade Barriers,* March 2010.

[4] The Andean Price Band system is applied by the four countries belonging to the Andean Community, a regional trade integration agreement formed by Bolivia, Colombia, Ecuador, and Peru. The four countries entered into the Andean Community as a form of trade integration through the removal of trade barriers and the application of common external tariffs, and a goal to eventually form a common market.

[5] USTR, *2010 National Trade Estimate Report on Foreign Trade Barriers,* March 2010.

Table 1. Colombian Tariff Rates on U.S. Exports

Tariff Base Rate (%)	Number of Tariff Lines	% of Total Tariff Lines
0	173	2.5
> 0 to 5	2,083	30.2
> 5 to 10	1,225	17.7
> 10 to 20	3,282	47.5
> 20 to 35	97	1.4
> 35	46	0.7
Total	**6,906**	**100.0**

Source: U.S.-Colombia Trade Promotion Agreement, Colombia Tariff Schedule, reported by United States International Trade Commission (USITC), *U.S.-Colombia Trade Promotion Agreement: Potential Economy-wide and Selected Sectoral Effects,* Investigation No. TA-2104-023, USITC Publication 3896, December 2006. Colombia Trade Promotion Agreement, Colombia Tariff Schedule.

Notes: Does not include tariff lines with base rate values of blanks. Total of 6,906 tariff lines includes 5,986 industrial and textile tariff lines and 920 agricultural tariff lines.

Review of the U.S.-Colombia Free Trade Agreement

Key CFTA Provisions[6]

The comprehensive free trade agreement will eventually eliminate tariffs and other barriers to goods and services. The agreement was reached after numerous rounds of negotiations over a period of nearly two years. Some issues that took longer to resolve were related to agriculture. Colombia had been seeking lenient agriculture provisions in the agreement, arguing that the effects of liberalization on rural regions could have adverse effects on smaller farmers and drive them to coca production. The United States agreed to give more sensitive sectors longer phase-out periods to allow Colombia more time to adjust to trade liberalization. Sectors receiving the longest phase-out periods include poultry and rice.

This section summarizes several key provisions in the original agreement text as provided by the United States Trade Representative (USTR), unless otherwise noted.[7]

Market Access

The agreement will provide for the elimination of tariffs on bilateral trade in eligible goods. Upon implementation, the agreement will eliminate 80% of duties on U.S. exports of consumer and

---

[6] The text of the U.S.-Colombia Free Trade Agreement (CFTA) is available online at the Office of the United States Trade Representative (USTR) website: http://www.ustr.gov.

[7] USTR, *Trade Facts,* "Free Trade with Colombia: Summary of the United States-Colombia Trade Promotion Agreement," June 2007.

industrial products to Colombia. An additional 7% of U.S. exports will receive duty-free treatment within five years of implementation and most remaining tariffs will be eliminated within 10 years after implementation.

Tariff Elimination and Phase-Outs

Upon entry into force, the CFTA will eliminate most tariffs immediately and phase out the remaining tariffs over periods of up to 19 years. Tariff elimination for major sectors include the following:

- Upon implementation of the agreement, more than 99% of U.S. and almost 76% of Colombian industrial and textile tariff lines will be free of duty. Virtually all industrial and textile tariff lines will be duty free 10 years after implementation.[8]

- All tariffs in textiles and apparel that meet the agreement's rules-of-origin provisions will be eliminated immediately (see section on "Textiles and Apparel" below).[9]

- Tariffs on agricultural products will be phased out over a period of time, ranging from three to 19 years (see section on "Agricultural Provisions" below). Colombia will eliminate quotas[10] and over-quota tariffs in 12 years for corn and other feed grains, 15 years for dairy products, 18 years for chicken leg quarters, and 19 years for rice.[11]

Agricultural Provisions

Colombia currently applies some tariff protection on all agricultural products. Upon implementation, the trade agreement will provide duty-free access on 77% of all agricultural tariff lines, accounting for 52% of current U.S. exports to Colombia. Colombia will eliminate most other tariffs on agricultural products within 15 years.[12] U.S. farm exports to Colombia that will receive immediate duty-free treatment include high-quality beef, cotton, wheat, soybeans, soybean meal, apples, pears, peaches, cherries, and many processed food products including frozen french fries and cookies. U.S. farm products that will receive improved market access include pork, beef, corn, poultry, rice, fruits and vegetables, processed products, and dairy products. The agreement will also provide duty-free tariff rate quotas on standard beef, chicken leg quarters, dairy products, corn, sorghum, animal feeds, rice, and soybean oil.[13]

Colombia's current price band system results in higher duties for certain U.S. exports to Colombia, including corn, wheat, rice, soybeans, pork, poultry, cheeses, and powdered milk. The

---

[8] United States International Trade Commission (USITC), *U.S.-Colombia Trade Promotion Agreement: Potential Economy-wide and Selected Sectoral Effects*, USITC Publication 3896, December 2006, pp. 2-1 and 2-2.

[9] Ibid.

[10] Tariff rate quotas are limits on the quantity of imports that can enter a country duty-free before tariff-rates are applied.

[11] United States Department of Agriculture (USDA), Foreign Agricultural Service, *Fact Sheet: U.S.-Colombia Trade Promotion Agreement Overall Agriculture Fact Sheet*, August 2008.

[12] Ibid.

[13] USTR, *Trade Facts: Free Trade with Colombia, Summary of the United States-Colombia Trade Promotion Agreement,"* June 2007.

CFTA will remove Colombia's price band system upon implementation of the agreement. However, if the rates under the price band system result in a lower rate than that given under the FTA, the United States will be allowed to sell the product to Colombia at the lower rates.[14]

Information Technology

Under the agreement, Colombia agreed to join the World Trade Organization's Information Technology Agreement (ITA), and remove its tariff and non-tariff barriers to information technology products. Colombia will allow trade in remanufactured goods, which is expected to increase export and investment opportunities for U.S. businesses involved in remanufactured products such as machinery, computers, cellular telephones, and other devices.

Textiles and Apparel

In textiles and apparel, products that meet the agreement's rules of origin requirements will receive duty-free and quota-free treatment immediately upon entry into force. The United States and Colombia have cooperation commitments under the agreement that allow for verification of claims of origin or preferential treatment, and denial of preferential treatment or entry if the claims cannot be verified. The rules of origin requirements are generally based on the yarn-forward standard to encourage production and economic integration. A "de minimis" provision will allow limited amounts of specified third-country content to go into U.S. and Colombian apparel to provide producers in both countries flexibility. A special textile safeguard will provide for temporary tariff relief if imports prove to be damaging to domestic producers.

Government Procurement

In government procurement contracts, the two countries agreed to grant non-discriminatory rights to bid on government contracts. These provisions cover the purchases of Colombia's ministries and departments, as well as its legislature and courts. U.S. companies would also be assured access to the purchases of a number of Colombia's government enterprises, including its oil company.

Services

In services trade, the two countries agreed to market access in most services sectors, with very few exceptions. Colombia agreed to exceed commitments made in the WTO and to remove significant services and investment barriers, such as requirements that U.S. firms hire nationals rather than U.S. citizens to provide professional services. Colombia also agreed to eliminate requirements to establish a branch in order to provide a service and unfair penalties imposed on U.S. companies for terminating their relationships with local commercial agents. U.S. financial service suppliers will have full rights to establish subsidiaries or branches for banks and insurance companies. Portfolio managers will be allowed to provide portfolio management services to both mutual funds and pension funds in the partner country, including to funds that manage privatized social security accounts.

---

[14] USITC Publication 3896, December 2006, p. 3-4.

Investment

Investment provisions will help establish a stable legal framework for foreign investors from the partner country. All forms of investment are to be protected, including enterprises, debt, concessions and similar contracts, and intellectual property. U.S. investors are to be treated as Colombian investors with very few exceptions. U.S. investors in Colombia will have substantive and procedural protections that foreign investors have under the U.S. legal system, including due process protections and the right to receive fair market value for property in the event of an expropriation. Protections for U.S. investments will be backed by a transparent, binding international arbitration mechanism. In the preamble of the agreement, the United States and Colombia agreed that foreign investors would not be accorded greater substantive rights with respect to investment protections than domestic investors under domestic law.[15]

IPR Protection

The agreement will provide intellectual property rights (IPR) protections for U.S. and Colombian companies. In all categories of IPR, U.S. companies are to be treated no less favorably than Colombian companies. In trademark protection, the agreement will require the two countries to have a system for resolving disputes about trademarks used in internet domain names; to develop an on-line system for the registration and maintenance of trademarks and have a searchable database; and to have transparent procedures for trademark registration.

In protection of copyrighted works, the agreement has a number of provisions for protection of copyrighted works in a digital economy, including provisions that copyright owners will maintain rights over temporary copies of their works on computers. Other agreement provisions include rights for copyright owners for making their work available on-line; extended terms of protection for copyrighted works; requirements for governments to use only legitimate computer software; rules on encrypted satellite signals to prevent piracy of satellite television programming; and rules for the liability of Internet service providers for copyright infringement.

In protection of patents and trade secrets, the CFTA will limit the grounds on which a country could revoke a patent, thus protecting against arbitrary revocation. In protection of test data and trade secrets, the agreement will protect products against unfair commercial use for a period of five years for pharmaceuticals and 10 years for agricultural chemicals. In addition, the agreement will require the establishment of procedures to prevent marketing of pharmaceutical products that infringe patents, and provide protection for newly developed plant varieties. The parties expressed their understanding that the intellectual property chapter would not prevent either party from taking measures to protect public health by promoting access to medicines for all.

On music and motion picture property piracy, the CFTA IPR provisions include penalties for piracy and counterfeiting and criminalize end-user piracy. It requires the parties to authorize the seizure, forfeiture, and destruction of counterfeit and pirated goods and the equipment used to produce them. The agreement will mandate both statutory and actual damages for copyright infringement and trademark piracy. This will ensure that monetary damages could be awarded even if a monetary value to the violation is difficult to assess.

---

[15] USTR, *Trade Facts: Free Trade with Colombia, Summary of the United States-Colombia Trade Promotion Agreement,* June 2007.

Customs Procedures and Rules of Origin

The agreement includes comprehensive rules of origin provisions to ensure that only U.S. and Colombian goods benefit from the agreement. The agreement also includes customs procedures provisions, including requirements for transparency and efficiency, procedural certainty and fairness, information sharing, and special procedures for the release of express delivery shipments.

Labor Provisions

The labor and worker rights obligations are included in the core text of the agreement. The United States and Colombia reaffirmed their obligations as members of the International Labor Organization (ILO). The two countries agreed to adopt, maintain and enforce laws that incorporate core internationally recognized labor rights, as stated in the 1998 ILO *Declaration on Fundamental Principles and Rights at Work*, including a prohibition on the worst forms of child labor. The parties also agreed to enforce labor laws with acceptable conditions of work, hours of work, and occupational safety and health. All obligations of the CFTA chapter on labor are subject to the same dispute settlement procedures and enforcement mechanisms as other chapters of the agreement.

The agreement includes procedural guarantees to ensure that workers and employers have fair, equitable, and transparent access to labor tribunals or courts. It has a labor cooperative and capacity building mechanism to pursue bilateral or regional cooperation activities, which may include the principles embodied in the 1998 ILO Declaration and activities to promote compliance with ILO Convention 182 on the Worst Forms of Child Labor. The United States and Colombia agreed to cooperate on activities on laws and practices related to ILO labor standards; the ILO convention on the worst forms of child labor; methods to improve labor administration and enforcement of labor laws; social dialogue and alternative dispute resolution; occupational safety and health compliance; and mechanisms and best practices on protecting the rights of migrant workers.

Environmental Provisions

The environmental obligations are included in the core text of the agreement. The agreement requires the United States and Colombia to effectively enforce their own domestic environmental laws and to adopt, maintain, and implement laws and all other measures to fulfill obligations under covered multilateral environmental agreements (MEAs). Both countries committed to pursue high levels of environmental protection and to not derogate from environmental laws in a manner that will weaken or reduce protections. The agreement includes procedural guarantees to ensure fair, equitable, and transparent proceedings for the administration and enforcement of environmental laws. In addition, the agreement includes provisions to help promote voluntary, market-based mechanisms to protect the environment and to ensure that views of civil society are appropriately considered through a public submissions process. All obligations in the environmental chapter of the agreement are subject to the same dispute settlement procedures and enforcement mechanisms as obligations in other chapters of the agreement.

Dispute Settlement

The core obligations of the agreement, including labor and environmental provisions, are subject to dispute settlement provisions. The agreement's provisions on dispute panel proceedings include language to help promote openness and transparency through open public hearings; public release of legal submissions by parties; and opportunities for interested third parties to submit views. The provisions require the parties to make every attempt, through cooperation and consultations, to arrive at a mutually satisfactory resolution of a dispute. If the parties are unable to settle the dispute through consultations, the complaining party will have the right to request an independent arbitral panel to help resolve the dispute. Possible outcomes could include monetary penalties or a suspension of trade benefits.

Labor and Environmental Provisions after May 10, 2007, Bipartisan Trade Framework

In early 2007, some Members of Congress indicated that some of the provisions in pending U.S. FTAs would have to be strengthened to gain their approval, particularly relating to core labor standards. After several months of negotiation, bipartisan Congressional leadership and the Bush Administration reached an understanding on May 10, 2007, on a new bipartisan trade framework that calls for the inclusion of internationally recognized labor rights and environmental provisions in the text of pending free trade agreements. On June 28, 2007, the United States reached an agreement with Colombia on legally binding amendments to the CFTA on labor, the environment, and other matters to reflect the bipartisan understanding of May 10.

The amendments to the FTA are similar to the amendments that were made to the U.S.-Peru free trade agreement, which was approved by Congress in December 2008. Some of the key amendments include obligations related to five basic ILO labor rights, multilateral environmental agreements (MEAs), and pharmaceutical intellectual property rights (IPR). These provisions would be enforceable through the FTA's dispute settlement mechanism. On October 30, 2007, the Colombian Senate "overwhelmingly" approved the labor and environmental amendments to the CFTA, marking the end of the approval process for the agreement in Colombia.[16]

Basic Labor Provisions

After the bipartisan agreement, the Administration reached an agreement with Colombia to amend the CFTA to require the parties to "adopt, maintain and enforce in their own laws and in practice" the five basic internationally recognized labor principles, as stated in the 1998 ILO Declaration. The amendments to the agreement strengthened the earlier labor provisions which only required the signatories to *strive* to ensure that their domestic laws would provide for labor standards consistent with internationally recognized labor principles.

The amendments that resulted from the bipartisan trade framework were intended to enhance the protection and promotion of worker rights by including enforceable ILO core labor principles in the agreement. These include (1) freedom of association; (2) the effective recognition of the right to collective bargaining; (3) the elimination of all forms of forced or compulsory labor; (4) the

---

[16] Rosella Brevetti, *International Trade Reporter*, "Colombian Senate Overwhelmingly Approves Labor-Related Amendments to FTA with U.S.," November 1, 2007.

effective abolition of child labor and a prohibition on the worst forms of child labor; and (5) the elimination of discrimination in respect of employment and occupation. These obligations would refer only to the 1998 ILO *Declaration on the Fundamental Principles and Rights at Work.* Another change to the agreement relates to labor law enforcement. A decision made by a signatory on the distribution of enforcement resources would not be a reason for not complying with the labor provisions. Under the amended provisions, parties would not be allowed to derogate from labor obligations in a manner affecting trade or investment. Labor obligations would be subject to the same dispute settlement, same enforcement mechanisms, and same criteria for selection of enforcement mechanisms as all other obligations in the agreement.

Provisions on Environment

In the original text of the agreement, the parties would have been required to "effectively enforce" their own domestic environmental laws; this was the only environmental provision that would have been enforceable through the agreement's dispute settlement procedures. Other environmental provisions in the original text that were not enforceable included provisions on environmental cooperation, procedural guarantees for enforcement of environmental laws, and provisions for a public submissions process. Under the amended version of the FTA, the United States and Colombia agreed to effectively enforce their own domestic environmental laws, *and* to adopt, maintain, and implement laws and all other measures to fulfill obligations under the seven covered multilateral environmental agreements (MEAs). The amended agreement states that *all* obligations in the environment chapter would be subject to the same dispute settlement procedures and enforcement mechanisms as all other obligations in the agreement.

Other Provisions

Other amendments to the FTA include provisions on intellectual property, government procurement, and port security. On intellectual property rights (IPR) protection, some Members of Congress were concerned that the original commitments would have impeded the entry of generic medicines to treat AIDS or other infectious diseases. The amended agreement was a way of trying to find a balance between the need for IPR protection for pharmaceutical companies to foster innovation and the desire for promoting access to generic medicines to all segments of the population. The amended text of the agreement maintains the five years of data exclusivity for test data related to pharmaceuticals. However, if Colombia relies on U.S. Federal Drug Administration (FDA) approval of a given drug, and meets certain conditions for expeditious approval of that drug in Colombia, the data exclusivity period would expire at the same time that the exclusivity expired in the United States. This could allow generic medicines to enter more quickly into the market in Colombia.

In government procurement, the amended provisions allow U.S. state and federal governments to condition government contracts on the adherence to the core labor laws in the country where the good is produced or the service is performed. Government agencies also will be allowed to include environmental protection requirements in their procurements. Concerning port security, an added provision ensures that if a foreign-owned company were to provide services at a U.S. port that would raise national security concerns, the CFTA would not be an impediment for U.S. authorities in taking actions to address those concerns.[17]

---

[17] Office of the United States Trade Representative, *Trade Facts,* "Bipartisan Trade Deal," Bipartisan Agreement on (continued...)

U.S.-Colombia Trade Relations

With a population of 48 million people, Colombia is the third-most populous country in Latin America, after Brazil and Mexico. Colombia's economy, the fourth-largest economy in Latin America, after Brazil, Mexico, and Argentina, is small when compared to the U.S. economy. Colombia's gross domestic product (GDP) in 2011 was estimated at $331 billion, about 2.2% of U.S. GDP of $15.1 trillion in 2011 (see **Table 2**). Colombia's exports of goods and services accounted for 18% of its GDP in 2011, while imports of goods and services accounted for 20%.

Table 2. Key Economic Indicators for Colombia and the United States

	Colombia		United States	
	2001	**2011**[a]	**2001**	**2011**[a]
Population (millions)	41	48	285	313
Nominal GDP ($US billions)[b]	98	331	10,286	15,094
GDP, PPP[c] Basis ($US billions)	246	472	10,286	15,094
Per Capita GDP ($US)	2,391	6,960	36,082	48,200
Per Capita GDP in $PPP[c]	5,984	9,920	36,082	48,200
Exports of goods and services (US$ billions)	15	60	1,028	2,086
Exports as % of GDP[d]	15%	18%	10%	14%
Imports of goods and services (US$ billions)	18	67	1,399	2,664
Imports as % of GDP[d]	19%	20%	14%	18%

Source: Compiled by CRS based on data from the Economist Intelligence Unit (EIU) on-line database.

a.   Most figures for 2011 are estimates.

b.   Nominal GDP is calculated by EIU based on figures from World Bank and World Development Indicators.

c.   PPP refers to purchasing power parity, which attempts to factor in price differences across countries when estimating the size of a foreign economy in U.S. dollars.

d.   Exports and Imports as % of GDP are derived by the EIU and include trade in both goods and services.

The United States is Colombia's dominant trading partner in both imports and exports. Subsequently, any change in U.S. demand for Colombian products can have a considerable effect on Colombia's economy. Colombia's market opening measures over the past 10 years, however, have resulted in changes to its direction of trade and the percentage of trade with the United States has been declining. Colombia has regional trade agreements with most countries in Latin America, including the Central America Northern Triangle (Guatemala, Honduras, and El Salvador); Mexico; Mercosur (Brazil, Argentina, Paraguay, and Uruguay); and Chile. An FTA with Canada, approved by both countries in 2010, entered into force on August 15, 2011. Colombia has also recently signed an FTA with the European Union, which is awaiting formal approval by both partners.

(...continued)

Trade Policy, May 2007, pp. 4-5.

The United States accounts for 25% of Colombia's total imports. China is the second-leading supplier of Colombia's imports, accounting for 15% of total imports in 2011, followed by Mexico, which accounted for 11%. The United States is also Colombia's leading export market, accounting for 38% of total Colombian exports in 2011. In agriculture, Argentina surpassed the United States as Colombia's leading supplier of agricultural imports in 2010. Argentina supplied 28% of Colombia's agricultural imports in 2010, up from 21% in 2009. In comparison, the United States supplied 25% of Colombia's agricultural imports in 2009 and 18% in 2010.

U.S.-Colombia Merchandise Trade

Colombia accounts for a very small percentage of U.S. total trade (1.0% in 2011). Colombia ranks 22nd among U.S. export markets and 23rd among foreign exporters to the United States. U.S. exports to Colombia totaled $12.8 billion in 2011, while U.S. imports totaled $22.4. As shown in **Table 3** the dominant U.S. import category from Colombia in 2010 was oil and gas (47%); followed by petroleum and coal products (15%); nonferrous metal (9%); fruits and tree nuts (6%); and basic chemicals (5%). The leading U.S. export category to Colombia was petroleum and coal products (21%); basic chemicals (9%); agriculture and construction machinery (9%); resin, synthetic rubber and products (4%); and general purpose machinery (4%).

Table 3. U.S. Trade with Colombia in 2011

U.S. Domestic Exports			U.S. Imports for Consumption		
Leading Items (NAIC 4 Digit Level)	$ Millions	Share	Leading Items (NAIC 4 Digit Level)	$ Millions	Share
Petroleum and coal products	2,677.5	21%	Oil and gas	10,605.1	47%
Basic chemicals	1,184.5	9%	Petroleum and coal products	3,457.6	15%
Agriculture and construction machinery	1,165.0	9%	Nonferrous metal	2,077.1	9%
Resin, synthetic rubber and products	559.7	4%	Fruits and tree nuts	1,382.48	6%
Other general purpose machinery	559.2	4%	Basic chemicals	1,193.16	5%
All other	6,683.62	52%	All other	3,675.5	18%
Total exports	12,829.6	—	Total imports	22,390.9	—

Source: Compiled by CRS using USITC Interactive Tariff and Trade DataWeb at http://dataweb.usitc.gov.

In 2011, U.S. imports from Colombia increased from $15.7 billion the previous year to $22.4 billion. In 2009 had declined 14%, from $13.1 billion in 2008 to $11.2 billion. In the five-year period prior to 2008, imports had been increasing steadily, from $6.3 billion to $13.1 billion in 2008. U.S. exports to Colombia also increased in 2011, from $11.0 billion in 2010 to $12.8 billion. In 2009, following international trends in global trade after the financial crisis, exports to Colombia decreased from $10.7 billion in 2008 to $8.8 billion. Between 2003 and 2008, U.S. exports to Colombia increased from $3.5 billion to $10.6 billion (see **Figure 1**). Prior to 2003, U.S. imports from and exports to Colombia fluctuated from year to year without very significant changes.

Figure 1. U.S. Trade with Colombia: 1996-2011

($ Billions)

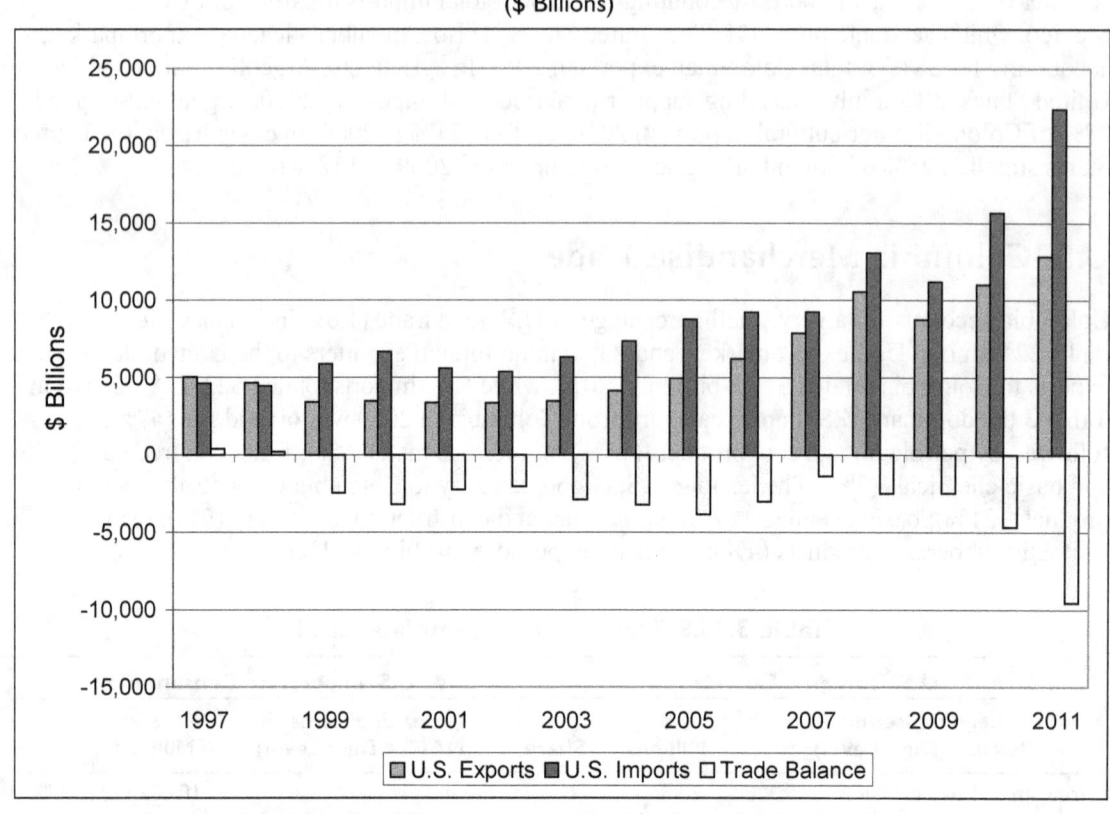

Source: Compiled by CRS using USITC Interactive Tariff and Trade DataWeb at http://dataweb.usitc.gov.

Andean Trade Preference Act

Under the Andean Trade Preference Act, a regional trade preference program, the United States extends duty-free treatment to imports from Colombia.[18] ATPA was enacted on December 4, 1991 (Title II of P.L. 102-182), and was renewed and modified under the Andean Trade Promotion and Drug Eradication Act (ATPDEA; Title XXXI of P.L. 107-210) on August 6, 2002. Additional products receiving preferential duty treatment under ATPDEA included certain items in the following categories: petroleum and petroleum products, textiles and apparel products, footwear, tuna in flexible containers, and others. Since the enactment of ATPDEA, Congress extended ATPA preferences several times for Colombia and other Andean countries for short periods of time. The most recent extension renewed preferences for Colombia and Ecuador until July 31, 2012. The previous extension of ATPA (P.L. 111-344) expired on February 12, 2011. It was not renewed until October 21, 2011, when Congress approved implementing legislation for the U.S.-Colombia Trade Promotion Agreement (P.L. 112-42), which extended trade preferences for Colombia and Ecuador until July 31, 2013 with a retroactive date of February 12, 2011.

---

[18] For more information see CRS Report RS22548, *ATPA Renewal: Background and Issues*, by M. Angeles Villarreal.

ATPA, as amended by ATPDEA, is part of a broader U.S. initiative with Andean countries to address the drug trade problem with Latin America. It authorizes the President to grant duty-free treatment or reduced tariffs to certain products from the list of beneficiary countries (Bolivia, Colombia, Ecuador, and Peru) that met domestic content and other requirements, as long as the country meets specific eligibility requirements. Bolivia is no longer a designated beneficiary country because it failed to meet the eligibility criteria, and Peru was not included in the most recent extension of ATPA because the U.S.-Peru FTA has entered into force. The act (as a complement to crop eradication, interdiction, military training, and other counter-narcotics efforts) was intended to promote economic growth in the Andean region and to encourage a shift away from dependence on illegal drugs by supporting legitimate economic activities. Increased access to the U.S. market was expected to help create jobs and expand legitimate opportunities for workers in the Andean countries in alternative export sectors.

In 2011, 55% of U.S. imports from Colombia (compared to 93% in 2010) received duty-free treatment through preference programs or normal trade relations (see **Table 4**). The lapse in the renewal of ATPA in 2011 resulted in a decline in ATPA imports in 2011 when only 12% of total U.S. imports entered the country under ATPA, compared to 60% in 2010. As shown in **Table 5**, leading ATPA imports in 2011 were: oil and gas; petroleum and coal products; mushrooms, nursery and related products (including cut flowers); apparel; and plastic products. The trade preference program contributed to a rapid increase in ATPA imports from Colombia. This increase was partially due to an increase in the volume of imports, but prices of oil and energy-related imports were also a major factor. Oil and gas products accounted for 77% of ATPA imports from Colombia in 2011.

Table 4. U.S. Imports from Colombia

($ Millions)

	2003	2004	2005	2006	2007	2008	2009	2010	2011
Total Imports	6,346.2	7,360.6	8,770.3	9,239.8	9,251.2	13,058.8	11,209.4	15,672.6	22,390.93
All Duty-Free	4,109.2	6557.8	7,892.5	8,531.5	8,447.1	12,044.1	9,962.9	14,536.6	12,224.8
% of Total	65%	89%	90%	92%	91%	92%	89%	93%	55%
ATPAa	2,908.7	3,888.9	4,653.2	4,791.2	4,527.7	7,339.2	5,589.5	9,472.6	2,674.6
% of Total	46%	53%	53%	52%	49%	56%	50%	60%	12%

Source: Compiled by CRS using USITC data.

a.   Includes imports under ATPA and ATPDEA.

Table 5. U.S. Imports from Colombia under ATPA

($ Millions)

Import Item[a]	2003	2004	2005	2006	2007	2008	2009	2010	2011
Oil and gas	1,692.9	2,299.7	2,897.1	3,183.7	3,152.6	5,813.9	4,318.2	7,914.3	2,066.4
Petroleum and coal products	321.2	405.5	454.6	202.5	141.2	375.3	249.0	363.4	245.9
Mushrooms, nursery and related products	343.3	415.0	418.5	449.3	506.2	499.3	506.0	549.0	206.4
Apparel	240.8	412.2	441.1	405.5	294.1	269.0	182.4	217.2	46.1
Plastics products	15.8	20.0	32.1	39.6	49.7	33.5	31.0	60.0	14.5
Other ATPA imports	294.7	336.5	409.8	510.6	383.9	348.2	302.9	368.7	95.3
Total ATPA[a]	2,908.7	3,888.9	4,653.2	4,791.2	4,527.7	7,339.2	5,589.5	9,472.6	2,674.6

Source: Compiled by CRS using USITC data

a.   NAIC 4-digt level.

b.   Includes imports under ATPA and ATPDEA.

U.S.-Colombia Bilateral Foreign Direct Investment

U.S. foreign direct investment in Colombia on a historical-cost basis totaled $6.6 billion in 2010 (see **Table 6**). The largest amount was in mining, which accounted for 39.7%, or $2.6 billion, of total U.S. FDI in Colombia in 2010. The second-largest amount, $2.0 billion (31.0% of total), was in manufacturing, followed by $551 million in finance and insurance.

Table 6. U.S. Direct Investment Position in Colombia

(Historical-cost Basis: 2010)

Industry	Amount (U.S.$ Millions)	% of Total
Mining	2,608	39.7%
Manufacturing	2,039	31.0%
Finance and Insurance	551	8.4%
Total	6,574	

Source: Bureau of Economic Analysis, International Economic Accounts.

The U.S.-Colombia FTA is expected to improve investor confidence in Colombia and will likely increase the amount of U.S. FDI in the country. Investors from other countries would also be expected to increase investment in Colombia as the FDI environment improves. According to one study, FDI in Colombia would have increased by more than $2 billion from 2007 through 2010 had the CFTA been implemented in 2007.[19]

Background on Colombia[20]

Colombia is a democratic nation with a bicameral legislature. In spite of its democratic tradition, Colombia has suffered from internal conflict for over 40 years. This conflict and drug violence present unique challenges to Colombia's institutions and threaten the human rights of Colombian citizens. An independent candidate, Alvaro Uribe, won the 2002 presidential elections, largely because of his aggressive plan to reduce violence in Colombia. President Uribe, who served two terms in office, retained widespread support throughout his presidency. Colombia continues to face serious challenges despite the progress it has made since the Uribe Administration. In the presidential election of June 2010, Juan Manuel Santos of the Partido de Unidad Nacional (Partido de la U) was elected president of Colombia with 69% of the vote. President Santos previously served as defense minister (2006-2009) under former President Uribe and in two prior governments as finance minister and minister of trade. Santos was sworn into office on August 7, 2010. On September 9, 2010, President Santos unveiled a new ambitious trade strategy aimed at increasing the value of Colombian exports by improving competitiveness, increasing market access to new markets, and providing more government support. The new strategy reflects President Santos' support of the U.S.-Colombia FTA and his desire to continue FTA negotiations with other countries.[21]

Internal Conflict

Colombia has a long tradition of civilian, democratic rule, yet has been plagued by violence throughout its history. The three major armed groups today are the Revolutionary Armed Forces of Colombia (FARC), the National Liberation Army (ELN), and the United Self-Defense Forces of Colombia (AUC). Although the AUC disbanded in 2006, it remains a designated foreign terrorist organization. The Colombian government has made significant achievements against terrorist leadership targets in Colombia. A 2009 report by the State Department states that Colombia has maintained and strengthened its "Democratic Security" strategy, which combines military, intelligence, police operations, and efforts to demobilize combatants. It also provides public services in rural areas previously dominated by armed groups. Kidnappings in Colombia by criminal groups significantly decreased in 2008.[22] The threat of extradition to the United States has been a strong weapon against drug traffickers and terrorists. In 2008, Colombia extradited a

---

[19] United States International Trade Commission (USITC), *U.S.-Colombia Trade Promotion Agreement: Potential Economy-wide and Selected Sectoral Effects,* Investigation No. TA-2104-023, USITC Publication 3896, December 2006, p. 7-3.

[20] This section is drawn from CRS Report RL32250, *Colombia: Background, U.S. Relations, and Congressional Interest,* by June S. Beittel.

[21] Global Insight, "Colombian President Unveils Trade Strategy," September 9, 2010.

[22] United States Department of State, Office of the Coordinator for Counterterrorism, *Country Reports on Terrorism 2008,* April 2009, pp. 11 and 155.

record 208 defendants to the United States for prosecution, most of which were Colombian nationals.[23]

Violence in Colombia has its roots in a lack of state control over much of Colombian territory, and a long history of poverty and inequality. The shift of cocaine production from Peru and Bolivia to Colombia in the 1980s increased drug violence, and provided a source of revenue for both guerrillas and paramilitaries. Conflicts between the Conservative and Liberal parties have existed for more than 100 years and have killed hundreds of thousands of Colombians. While a power-sharing agreement between the Liberal and Conservative parties ended a civil war in 1957, it did not address the root causes of the violence. Numerous leftist guerrilla groups inspired by the Cuban Revolution formed in the 1960s as a response to state neglect and poverty. Rightwing paramilitaries were formed in the 1980s to defend landowners, many of them drug traffickers, against guerrillas. Most of the rightist paramilitary groups were coordinated by the AUC, which disbanded in 2006 after more than 30,000 of its members demobilized. The AUC has been accused of gross human rights abuses and collusion with the Colombian Armed Forces in their fight against the FARC and ELN. The AUC also participated in narcotics trafficking.

Human Rights Issues

The debate on U.S. policy toward Colombia and on the free trade agreement with Colombia has brought attention to allegations of human rights abuses by the FARC and ELN, paramilitary groups, and the Colombian Armed Forces. Congress has annually required that the Secretary of State certify to Congress that the Colombian military and policy forces are severing their links to the paramilitaries, investigating complaints of abuses, and prosecuting those who have had credible charges made against them. In its certification issued in September 2010, the State Department determined and certified to Congress that the Colombian government and armed forces are meeting statutory criteria related to human rights. The report states that though there continues to be a need for improvement, the Colombian government has taken positive steps to improve respect for human rights in the country. According to the report, the Colombian government's firm resolve on not tolerating extrajudicial killings has led to a rapid reversal in this trend. The report also acknowledges the significant steps that the Santos Administration has taken to demonstrate it is taking human rights seriously and its actions on a the establishment of a roundtable on labor, meetings with NGOs and civil society groups, increasing engagement with these groups, and outreach to Colombia's courts to repair relations with the judicial system.[24]

The February 2011 United Nations High Commissioner for Human Rights (UNHCHR) report recognized the commitment to human rights expressed by the Santos Administration during its first months in office and recognized several positive steps that the government of Colombia has taken in the protection of human rights. It also recognized, however, that internal armed conflict in Colombia, in particular that from guerrilla groups, continues to breach international humanitarian law.[25] The report from the previous year acknowledged the spirit of cooperation between the Colombian government and UNHCHR-Colombia, and the commitment of the government to address human rights challenges. As in previous reports, UNHCHR expressed

---

[23] Ibid, p. 164.

[24] U.S. State Department, Office of the Spokesman, *Determination and Certification of the Colombian Government and Armed Forces with Respect to Human Rights Related Conditions,* September 15, 2010.

[25] United Nations General Assembly-Human Rights Council, "Report of the United Nations High Commissioner for Human Rights on the situation of human rights in Colombia," February 3, 2011.

concerns about the activities and abuses committed by paramilitary forces that have rearmed, and by the FARC. The report described the continued vulnerability of groups like women, children, Afro-Colombians, the indigenous, journalists, union leaders, and human rights workers.[26]

U.S. Policy Toward Colombia

The focus of U.S. foreign policy toward Colombia has been to assist in curbing narcotics production and trafficking. The United States also seeks to promote democracy and economic development in order to strengthen regional security. The country is known for a long tradition of democracy but has had to contend with continuing violence from leftist guerrilla insurgencies dating from the 1960s and persistent drug trafficking activity. Plan Colombia, a multi-year effort to address Colombia's key challenges, has been the centerpiece of U.S. policy toward Colombia since 2000.

The United States has made a significant commitment of funds and material support to help Colombia and the Andean region fight drug trafficking since the development of Plan Colombia in 1999. In support of the plan, Congress passed legislation providing $1.3 billion in assistance for FY2000 (P.L. 106-246) and has provided more than $7 billion to support Plan Colombia from FY2000 through FY2010 in both State Department and Defense Department accounts. Since 2002, Congress has granted the State Department expanded authority to use counternarcotics funds for a unified campaign to fight both drug trafficking and terrorist organizations in Colombia. In 2004, Congress raised the statutory cap on U.S. personnel allowed to be deployed to Colombia in support of Plan Colombia. The three main illegally armed groups in Colombia participate in drug production and trafficking and have been designated foreign terrorist organizations by the State Department.[27]

Colombian Action Plan Related to Labor Rights

The United States and Colombia negotiated to develop an "Action Plan Related to Labor Rights" (the Action Plan) to help resolve the following U.S. concerns related to labor-related issues in Colombia: alleged violence against Colombian labor union members; inadequate efforts to bring perpetrators of violence to justice; and insufficient protection of workers' rights in Colombia. The governments of the United States and Colombia announced the plan on April 7, 2011. It includes numerous specific commitments from Colombian government to address U.S. concerns. The Obama Administration's announcement of the plan stated that the successful implementation of key elements of the plan will be a precondition for the agreement to enter into force.[28] The plan lists several obligations with several target dates throughout 2011, and with a final target date of 2014 for the completion of hiring extra labor inspectors. The most significant target dates were April 22, 2011 and June 15, 2011.

---

[26] Ibid.

[27] For more information on Plan Colombia and U.S. foreign assistance, see CRS Report RL32250, *Colombia: Background, U.S. Relations, and Congressional Interest*, by June S. Beittel.

[28] The White House, Office of the Press Secretary, "Leveling the Playing Field: Labor Protections and the U.S.-Colombia Trade Promotion Agreement," April 6, 2011, available at http://www.whitehouse.gov/the-press-office/2011/04/06/fact-sheets-us-colombia-trade-agreement-and-action-plan.

Details of the Action Plan

This section summarizes the details of the Action Plan, which can be found on the website of the Office of the United States Trade Representative (USTR).[29]

Creation of a Labor Ministry

One of Colombia's commitments under the Action Plan was to create a new Labor Ministry. On October 31, 2011, President Santos announced the appointment of Liberal Party leader Rafael Pardo to lead the country's newly formed Labor Ministry, with the goal of implementing a broader and more effective regime to protect labor rights. The Colombian government expects that the Labor Ministry will provide the framework to mobilize resources and strengthen enforcement of labor laws. During the Uribe Administration, Colombia's labor-related functions were managed under the Ministry of Social Protection (MSP), which was created in 2002 by President Alvaro Uribe. The MSP combined Colombia's Ministry of Health and Ministry of Labor into one central agency.

The Action Plan includes target dates for the measures related to the labor ministry, beginning on April 22, 2011, and ending on December 15, 2011.[30] The Action Plan lists the following as part of the Colombian government's commitments:

- Plan and budget for the hiring of 480 new labor inspectors over a four-year period, which will include the hiring of at least 100 new labor inspectors during 2011 and budgeting for an additional 100 new inspectors in the 2012 budget.

- Improve the system for citizens to file complaints concerning labor rights violations. The system includes a toll-free telephone hotline and a new web-based mechanism for registering complaints. The MSP will conduct outreach to promote awareness of the complaint mechanisms.

- Improve the MSP's mediation and conflict resolution system in all 32 departments (Colombian states) by assigning specialized resources to the MSP's regional offices, training workers and employers in conflict resolution, and conducting outreach. The MSP will also conduct outreach to the public, employers, and workers through TV programs and printed material.

Criminal Code Reform

The Colombian government submitted legislation to the Colombian Congress to reform the country's criminal code by establishing criminal penalties for employers that undermine the right to organize and bargain collectively. The new article in the criminal code encompasses a wide

---

[29] *Colombian Action Plan Related to Labor Rights,* April 7, 2011, available at http://www.ustr.gov.

[30] On April 6, 2011, the Colombian Congress overwhelmingly approved to split three fused ministries and grant President Juan Manuel Santos extraordinary powers over the following six months to restructure parts of the Colombian government. President Santos has six months to divide the three ministries and reconstruct certain departments. The new ministries will be: Interior, Justice and the Law, Health and Social Protection, Labor, Environment and Sustainable Development, and Housing, Cities, and Territory.

range of practices that adversely affect fundamental labor rights and would penalize violators with up to five years of imprisonment. The Colombian government committed to have the legislation enacted by the Colombian Congress by June 15, 2011.

Cooperatives

The Colombian government agreed to accelerate the effective date of the provisions of Article 63 of the 2010 Law of Formalization and First Employment, passed in December 2010. This provision of the law prohibits the misuse of cooperatives or any other kind of labor relationship that affects labor rights, and imposes significant fines for violations. The government submitted legislation to the Colombian Congress to move the effective date from July 1, 2013 to June 15, 2011. The Colombian congress approved the bill.

The Labor Ministry will direct 50 of the 100 new labor inspectors referenced above to be assigned exclusively to cases involving cooperatives. The hiring and training of these inspectors was to be completed by December 15, 2011. Most of these inspectors had been hired as of early December 2011. A second group of 50 labor inspectors specializing in cooperatives will be hired during 2012. The priority sectors for labor inspections will be the palm oil, sugar, mines, ports, and flower sectors. The Colombian government agreed to confirm to the U.S. government by April 22, 2011, that these inspections had begun.

The Colombian government agreed to issue regulations implementing the 2010 cooperatives law by June 15, 2011. The regulations are expected to:

- clarify earlier cooperatives laws;

- ensure coherence among these laws and the new cooperatives law;

- increase inspections of cooperatives;

- increase sanctions for labor law violators;

- strictly apply and enforce the requirements that cooperatives be autonomous and self-governing; and

- develop and conduct an outreach program to inform and advise workers of the following: their rights under Colombian law; remedies and courses of action available to them through the courts in order to enforce recognition of a direct employment relationship; and the existence of criminal penalties for employers who are responsible for undermining the right to organize and bargain collectively (upon congressional approval of the criminal code reforms in Colombia).

The Colombian government agreed to work with the U.S. government to ensure that the agreed objectives are addressed and provide quarterly reports on the enforcement results to all interested parties.

Temporary Service Agencies

The Colombian government committed to implement a regime to prevent the use of temporary service agencies to circumvent labor rights. This was to be done through actions such as improving the inspection process, designing a new training program for labor inspectors, and building databases to identify regions and sectors where there have been abuses. The enforcement regime was also to include a monitoring and reporting mechanism in which all interested parties could verify progress and compliance with labor laws. As a first step, the Labor Ministry was to issue quarterly reports for interested parties that include the results of preventive inspections, penalties, fines, the cancellation of licenses and permits, and the list of those agencies found to be in violation. The Colombian government agreed that the Labor Ministry would: share a draft of the enforcement plan with the U.S. government by April 22, 2011; work with the U.S. government to ensure that the agreed upon objectives are addressed; conduct a series of preventive inspections by June 15, 2011; and fully implement the enforcement plan by December 15, 2011.

Collective Pacts

The Colombian government committed to include in the bill on criminal code reform a provision stating it is a crime, subject to imprisonment, to use collective pacts to undermine the right to organize and bargain collectively. The provision would prohibit collective pacts from extending better conditions to non-union workers. The MSP, or the Labor Ministry, once it was created, would conduct a public outreach campaign to promote awareness, after approval of the criminal code reform in June 2011. The campaign is to run through 2011 and the Colombian government committed to budget additional resources for 2012. Colombia's Labor Ministry will enforce the reforms through preventive inspections and the new labor complaint mechanisms to detect and prosecute violations. The Colombian government also will request technical assistance from the International Labor Organization (ILO) to monitor the use of collective pacts and will work with the U.S. government to ensure that the agreed objectives are addressed.

Essential Services

Colombia agreed that the MSP, or the Labor Ministry, will collect the body of Colombian doctrine, case law, and jurisprudence that has narrowed the definition of essential services. The MSP was disseminated this information and relevant guidelines to labor inspectors, the judicial branch, unions, and employers by the target date of April 22, 2011.[31]

ILO Office

The Colombian government stated that it would request cooperation, advice, and technical assistance from the ILO to help in the implementation measures in the Action Plan. The Colombian government committed to work with the ILO to strengthen the presence and expand the capacity and role of the ILO in Colombia. The U.S. and Colombian governments committed to working together to identify the necessary resources and sources of support. The Colombian government's formal request to the ILO was accomplished by the target date of September 15, 2011.

---

[31] These documents are under review by the Office of the United States Trade Representative.

Protection Programs

Colombia's Ministry of Interior and Justice issued a Ministerial Resolution, by the target date of April 22, 2011, to broaden the scope of the definition of who is covered by its protection program. The broader definition includes: 1) labor activists; 2) persons who are engaged in active efforts to form a union; and 3) former unionists who are under threat because of their past activities. The Colombian government planned and budgeted for necessary additional resources for this expansion by increasing the FY2011 allocation by 50% (approximately US $6 million) to provide adequate support for the expansion in the protection program. For FY2012, the Colombian government assessed the level of funding necessary to support the program and presented the requested budget to the Colombian Congress before the target date of July 30, 2011.

The Ministry of Interior and Justice committed to eliminate the backlog of risk assessments on union member applications for protection, by July 30, 2011, through an emergency plan that had begun earlier. After the backlog elimination, the Colombian government committed to a national policy on conducting risk assessments to comply with the law to process all risk assessments within a 30-day period. On May 1, 2011, the Colombian government committed to providing monthly updates to interested parties.

The Colombian government committed to issue a decree to reform the scope and functioning of the interagency committee that reviews risk assessments by September 15, 2011. The new committee was to include representatives from the Inspector General's Office and the Public Defender's Office to enhance objectivity in the assessment process. The Colombian government agreed to share with the U.S. government the relevant parts of the draft decree by April 22, 2011, and agreed to work with the U.S. government to ensure that the agreed objectives are addressed. The Colombian government also committed to strengthen the existing protection system by immediately implementing administrative measures.

Colombia agreed to amend its teacher relocation and protection program, contained in Resolution 1240 (*Resolución 1240)* of 2010, to ensure that meritorious requests are granted to teachers and to eliminate sanctions against teachers not found to be under extraordinary risk. The Colombian government agreed to work with the U.S. government to ensure that the program is achieving the objective of effectively protecting those covered by it and to ensure that the agreed objectives are addressed. Colombia began the sharing of quarterly reports on the program with interested parties beginning July 1, 2011.

Criminal Justice Reform

The Colombian government agreed to assign 95 additional full-time judicial police investigators to exclusively support prosecutors investigating criminal cases involving union members and activists. The first 50 of these judicial police were assigned by June 30, 2011, and the remaining 45 were assigned by December 15, 2011. The government stated that it would respond favorably to a budget request from the Prosecutor General's office to increase funding for necessary resources to reduce impunity and for implementing the Action Plan. The Prosecutor General agreed to submit the budget request by May 20, 2011.

The Prosecutor General's Office of Colombia informed the Colombian government of numerous actions it had taken or plans to take to combat impunity in cases involving union members and labor activists:

- Issued a directive requiring criminal investigators to determine whether a victim was a union member or labor activist in the initial phase of the investigation;

- Issued a directive to the chiefs of the Unit of Justice and Peace and the Unit of Human Rights to share evidence and information about criminal cases involving union members, labor activists, teachers, journalists, and human rights activists;

- Developed a plan and identified budgetary needs for training judicial police investigators and prosecutors on crime scene management, and in investigative techniques with specific reference to the issues involved in labor cases; worked with the U.S. government in developing a detailed training program;

- Developed a plan and specified budgetary needs by May 20, 2011, to strengthen the institutional capacity, number of prosecutors and number of judicial police investigators;

- Finalized an analysis by July 15, 2011, on closed cases of homicides of union members and activists, in order to extract lessons that could improve investigations and prosecutions in future cases; the results of this analysis were widely publicized to help reduce impunity and deter future crimes;

- Developed a plan and identified specific budgetary needs for victims' assistance centers specialized in human rights cases, including labor cases; the Prosecutor General's Office agreed to staff the centers with professionals with expertise on human rights and labor issues; Colombia agreed to share the plans and budgetary allocations for this project to the U.S. government by June 15, 2011;

- Developed a program by the Prosecutor General's Office to address the backlog of unionist homicide cases that included: a) meeting with representatives of the union confederations and the National Labor School, *Escuela Nacional Sindical* (ENS), an independent labor rights monitoring body, in order to try to reconcile discrepancies; and b) internal guidance to prosecutors to accelerate action on cases with leads, with a special focus on "priority labor cases", and to provisionally close cold cases by June 15, 2011; and

- Improved public reporting of completed criminal cases involving labor violence by the Prosecutor General's Office through the following: a) publication by April 22, 2011, of cases decided as of January 1, 2011, and thereafter; and b) identification of methods by June 15, 2011, for posting information regarding all completed cases on the Prosecutor General's Office website.

Follow-Up Mechanism

The U.S. and Colombian governments agreed to assess progress in implementing the Action Plan and agreed to meet on a periodic basis through 2013 at the technical level and at the senior officials level.

Colombia's Commitments and Cooperation with the United States

The Action Plan includes numerous commitments on the part of the Colombian government that are part of its ongoing efforts to increase security and protection of union members, labor activists, and human rights defenders. It also includes new commitments to address U.S. concerns about the FTA. For example, since 2004, Colombia had been taking numerous measures to address the issue of worker rights abuses in the work arrangements known as cooperatives, but it also agreed to a new commitment under the Action Plan to accelerate the implementation date by two years of the cooperatives law passed in December 2010 under the Santos Administration. President Santos had promised to dismantle the role of cooperatives as labor intermediaries and increase protection of worker rights within the cooperatives during his campaign for president.[32]

The Colombian government has been committed to improving the security situation in Colombia since the Pastrana Administration (1998-2002) when Plan Colombia started. Some observers may view Colombia's commitments under the Action Plan as a continuation of Colombia's commitment to improve security and protection of its citizens with more of an emphasis on labor and human rights. Former Colombian President Alvaro Uribe (2002 to 2010) took numerous measures to increase the security situation in Colombia under Plan Colombia. This included close cooperation with the United States in providing security assistance in the form of equipment and training for the Colombian security forces or Colombian National Police and military as well as efforts to promote development and rule of law programs. Colombia's current President Juan Manuel Santos, who was inaugurated on August 7, 2010, pledged to continue the successful security strategies of his predecessor while pursuing democratic, economic, and social reforms. President Santos and his Vice President Angelino Garzón have promoted a more rigorous protection of human rights and have placed a greater emphases on denouncing threats against human rights defenders than previous governments.[33]

---

[32] *Escuela Nacional Sindica (ENS)*, "Trade Unions Comment on Government Proposal to Dismantle Associated-Work Cooperatives (Cooperativas de trabajo asociado), November 26, 2010.

[33] CRS Report RL32250, *Colombia: Background, U.S. Relations, and Congressional Interest*, by June S. Beittel.

Colombia's Actions in Meeting Milestones
As Reported by the Office of the United States Trade Representative (USTR)

Major Actions Taken by April 22, 2011

Began hiring 100 additional labor inspectors and budgeted for the hiring of 100 more labor inspectors in 2012.

Improved systems for citizens to file labor-related complaints via phone or internet.

Implemented an inspection system to detect improper use of temporary service agencies to circumvent labor rights and developed an enforcement plan to prevent abuses.

Established enforcement regime to detect and prosecute the use of collective pacts to undermine worker rights.

Began workshops to train labor inspectors and other government personnel in conflict resolution and launched a related outreach program to the public, employers, and workers.

Expanded government protection program and increased funding to provide protection for labor activists, workers who are trying to organize or join a union, and former unionists who are under threat because of past activities.

Strengthened the teacher relocation and protection program.

Mandated early identification in all new homicide cases of whether the victim was a union member or activist.

Developed a plan for training judicial police investigators and prosecutors on cases involving unionists.

Improved public reporting of completed cases by posting labor violence cases on the Prosecutor General's website.

Began process to reconcile discrepancies in the number of outstanding unionist homicide cases.

Major Actions Taken by June 15, 2011

Obtained congressional approval of legislation to establish a new Labor Ministry.

Obtained congressional approval of legislation to establish criminal penalties for employers undermining labor rights.

Enacted legal provisions prohibiting the misuse of cooperatives or other types of labor relationships.

Issued regulations implementing a new cooperatives law, including provisions to clarify earlier cooperatives laws, ensure coherence among these laws, and impose significant fines for companies violating these laws.

Launched a public outreach program to inform workers of their labor rights, with a focus on the new laws governing cooperatives; criminal anti-union conduct and abuse of collective pacts; and courses of action available to workers.

Developed and disseminated legal information regarding definition of essential services, especially with regard to laws establishing a public service as essential and exempt from the right to strike.

Reduced by 75% the backlog of risk assessments for unionists applying for the government protection program.

Issued internal guidance to prosecutors to accelerate action on cases with leads, especially those related to labor.

Developed a plan to strengthen the institutional capacity in regional offices of the Prosecutor General.

Developed a plan and identified budgetary needs for victims' assistance centers, including labor cases.

Submitted a budget request for the necessary government resources to end impunity and implement the Action Plan.

Developed a methodology for public posting of information regarding completed criminal cases involving labor.

Major Actions Taken by September 15, 2011

Completed an analysis by the Prosecutor General's Office of closed homicide cases of unionists for the purpose of extracting lessons to improve the investigation and prosecution of future cases.

Formally submitted a request for technical assistance to the ILO for implementation of Action Plan measures.

Eliminated the backlog of risk assessments for applicants to the protection program for union members and activists.

Completed the reassignment of 50 judicial police investigators to criminal cases involving unionists.

Remaining Commitments

Obtained final approval of the 2012 budget, including funding for 100 additional labor inspectors.

Completed hiring of almost 100 new labor inspectors and assignment of new judicial police investigators; completed first round of training for inspectors in alternative dispute resolution; and implemented temporary service agency enforcement plan.

Hiring of an additional 380 labor inspectors to be completed by the end of 2014.

Source: USTR, *Colombia Action Plan Related to Labor Rights: Accomplishments to Date,* at http://www.ustr.gov.

Responses to the Action Plan in Colombia

Since the announcement of the Action Plan, at least two of Colombia's labor confederations responded favorably to working with the Santos Administration and with business representatives to come to an agreement on labor issues. Labor unions in Colombia have responded favorably to at least some elements that were included in the Action Plan, especially those related to work cooperatives. The Secretary General of Colombia's National Labor Confederation, Julio Roberto Gómez, remarked in November 2010 that President Santos' proposal under the 2010 labor cooperatives law was a "great achievement" for the trade union movement in Colombia.[34]

Initial responses to the Action Plan from Colombian unions were mostly favorable, but some labor unions continue to oppose the FTA with the United States. The ENS stated that the Action Plan was the most significant advance for the labor movement in Colombia in twenty years, but has also stated that it has gaps, such as not going far enough to address the labor abuses that are occurring in labor cooperatives.[35] The Solidarity Center in the Andean Region contends that Colombia has not met its full commitment in the Action Plan to implement the 2010 Cooperatives Law because the decree that was signed in June 2011 is only a "partial decree." The Center argues that the decree leaves out other forms of contracting, other than cooperatives, that are included in the original decree.[36] Some unions continue to oppose the FTA with the United States. Public sector unionists, in particular, protested plans of the Colombian and U.S. governments to enter into the FTA, even while the two presidents met in Washington, DC, on April 7, 2011, to announce the agreement on the Action Plan.

On May 26, 2011, a tripartite labor agreement was reached among representatives of the Colombian government, the private sector, and some labor representatives. The agreement, which is the first concluded since June 2006, includes a consensus to request the ILO to provide cooperation, advice, and technical assistance on the implementation of the Action Plan measures. Two of Colombia's major labor confederations, however, the Confederation of Workers of Colombia (CTC) and the Central Union of Workers (CUT), did not sign the agreement because they felt they did not have sufficient time to analyze the agreement or to put forth their own proposals in the agreement. Two other confederations, the General Labor Confederation (CGT) and the Colombian Pensioners Confederation (CPC) signed the agreement and stated that it was one of the most significant advances in many years in strengthening labor movement in Colombia.[37]

---

[34] ENS, "Trade Unions Comment on Government Proposal to Dismantle Associated-Work Cooperatives (Cooperativas de trabajo asociado), November 26, 2010.

[35] In-person interview with ENS on June 1, 2011.

[36] Solidarity Center for Andean Region, June 16, 2011.

[37] ENS, "Labor Agreement: CGT and CPC signed it, the CTC and the CUT did not sign it but presented proposals," June 1, 2011.

Issues for Congress

Economic Impact

Policymakers have expressed a general interest in the potential impact of the agreement on bilateral trade and on the U.S. and Colombian economies. Upon full implementation, the U.S.-Colombia FTA will likely have a small, but positive, net economic effect on the United States. The net effect is expected to be minimal because Colombia's economy is very small when compared to the U.S. economy (1.6%) and the value of U.S. trade with Colombia is a very small percentage of overall U.S. trade. Most of the economy-wide trade effects of trade liberalization from the FTA will likely arise from Colombia's removal of tariff barriers and other trade restrictions. Approximately 90% of U.S. imports from Colombia enter the United States duty-free, either unconditionally or under the ATPA or other U.S. provisions; hence, the marginal effects of the FTA on the U.S. economy likely will not be significant.

Study Findings on Economic Impact

A study by the United States International Trade Commission (USITC) assessed the potential effects of a U.S.-Colombia FTA on the U.S. economy. The study found that, in general, the primary impact of an FTA with Colombia would be increased U.S. exports to Colombia as a result of enhanced U.S. access to the Colombian market.[38] Major findings of the USITC study on the likely effects of a U.S.-Colombia FTA on the U.S. economy, should the agreement be fully implemented, include the following:[39]

- U.S. exports to Colombia would increase by $1.1 billion (13.7%) and U.S. imports from Colombia would increase by $487 million (5.5%). U.S. GDP would increase by over $2.5 billion (less than 0.05%).

- The largest estimated increases in U.S. exports to Colombia, by value, would be in chemical, rubber, and plastic products; machinery and equipment; and motor vehicles and parts. In terms of percentage increases, the largest increases in U.S. exports would be in rice and dairy products.

- The largest estimated increases in U.S. imports from Colombia, by value, would be in sugar and crops not elsewhere classified. The largest estimated increases in U.S. imports, by percent, would be in dairy products and sugar.

- On an industry level, the FTA would result in minimal to no effect on output or employment for most sectors of the U.S. economy. The U.S. sugar sector would be the only sector with an estimated decline of more than 0.1% in output or employment. The largest increases in U.S. output and employment would be in the processed rice, cereal grains, and wheat sectors.

---

[38] United States International Trade Commission (USITC), *U.S.-Colombia Trade Promotion Agreement: Potential Economy-wide and Selected Sectoral Effects,* Investigation No. TA-2104-023, USITC Publication 3896, December 2006. (Hereinafter USITC, December 2006).

[39] USITC, December 2006, pp. 2-1 and 2-2.

The USITC reviewed seven studies that it found on the probable economic effects of a U.S.-Colombia FTA.[40] The results of the studies reviewed by USITC varied. One study found that U.S. exports to Colombia would increase by 2.4% to 8.3%, while another study assessed that the expected increase would be 44%. Two studies found that the largest increases in U.S. exports would be in agriculture products, metal and wood, and food products. In assessing the impact on U.S. imports from Colombia, the results of the studies also varied. One study found that U.S. imports from Colombia would increase by 2.0% to 6.2%, while another found that U.S. imports would increase by 37%. The largest increases would be in apparel and leather goods, textile products, and metal and wood. The studies also assessed that an FTA would result in small overall welfare gains for both the United States and Colombia and a positive impact on the U.S. agricultural sector despite an increase in U.S. sugar imports.[41]

The non-governmental Institute for International Economics (IIE) did a study in 2006 assessing the possible impact of a U.S.-Colombia FTA on both the U.S. and Colombian economies.[42] The study found that a U.S.-Colombia FTA would be expected to result in an increase in total trade between the two countries. The total value of U.S. imports from Colombia would increase by an estimated 37% while the value of U.S. exports to Colombia would increase by an estimated 44%.[43] In terms of welfare gains, the study assessed that a U.S.-Colombia FTA would result in small welfare benefits for both partners, though the gains would be larger for Colombia. On a sectoral level, the study found that an agreement would have a minor sectoral effect on the U.S. economy, but the effect would be more significant for Colombia because it is the smaller partner. The study indicated that Colombia would face certain structural adjustment issues with a displacement of low-skilled workers in some sectors, but that these workers would all be able to find job possibilities in the expanding sectors.[44]

One of the drawbacks to a bilateral free trade agreement is that it may result in trade diversion because it is not fully inclusive of all regional trading partners.[45] Trade diversion results when a country enters into an FTA and then shifts the purchase of goods or services (imports) from a country that is not an FTA partner to a country that is an FTA partner even though it may be a higher cost producer. In the case of the United States and Colombia, for example, goods from the United States may replace Colombia's lower-priced imports from other countries in Latin America. If this were to happen, the United States would now be the producer of that item, not because it produces the good more efficiently, but because it is receiving preferential access to the

---

[40] In its review of the seven economic studies, the USITC noted that these studies analyzed a proposed, possible, or hypothetical U.S.-Colombia free trade agreement (FTA) and not the final text of the actual FTA that was the subject of its investigation. Therefore, the underlying assumptions made in the reviewed studies may be different than those of the USITC's analysis.

[41] USITC, December 2006, pp. 7-1 to 7-4.

[42] Jeffrey J. Schott, editor, Institute for International Economics (IIE), *Trade Relations Between Colombia and the United States,* August 2006. (Hereinafter IIE, August 2006).

[43] IIE August 2006, Chapter 4, "Potential Benefits of a U.S.-Colombia FTA," by Dean A. DeRosa and John P. Gilbert. This chapter uses empirical and applied methods of economic analysis to examine the potential quantitative impact of a U.S.-Colombia FTA and is one of the studies reviewed by the USITC in its assessment of a U.S.-Colombia FTA.

[44] Ibid, p. 112.

[45] When a trade agreement lowers trade barriers on a good, production may shift from domestic producers to lower cost foreign producers and result in substituting an imported good for the domestic good. This process is called trade creation. Trade creation provides economic benefits as consumers have a wider choice of goods and services available at lower costs. Trade creation also results in adjustment costs, however, usually in the form of domestic job losses as production shifts to another country.

Colombian market. The IIE study assessed that a CFTA probably would not cause trade diversion in the United States, but that it could cause some trade diversion in Colombia. The IIE study estimated that an FTA with the United States would result in a decrease in Colombia's imports from other countries of approximately 9%.[46]

Possible Economic Impact on Agricultural Sector

The USITC study found that one of the impacts of a U.S.-Colombia FTA would be increased U.S. agriculture exports to Colombia as a result of enhanced U.S. access to the Colombian market.[47] In the agricultural sector, key findings of the study include the following:

- The removal of tariff and nontariff barriers would likely result in a higher level of U.S. exports of meat (beef and pork) to Colombia. U.S. imports of meat from Colombia would eventually increase, but are currently restricted by Colombia's lack of certification to export fresh, chilled, or frozen beef or pork to the United States.

- Colombia's elimination of trade barriers and certain government support measures under a CFTA would likely result in increased U.S. grain exports to Colombia. Rice would account for most of the increase, with yellow corn and wheat accounting for the remaining balance.

- U.S. exports to Colombia in soybeans, soybean products, and animal feeds would likely increase under a CFTA.[48]

According to the IIE study, the main gains to Colombia in agricultural trade would likely be more secure and preferential market access to the U.S. market. U.S. agricultural exports would gain a small but not insignificant preference in the Colombian market for temperate-zone agricultural produce. The study's authors state that the long time periods for phasing out tariffs for sensitive products and safeguard provisions that would replace Colombia's price band system would lessen the impact of increased imports from the United States. One section of the study describes the results of a global applied general equilibrium model on the pending FTA. In terms of the overall effects on Colombia's economy, the results of the study imply that, in the medium term, Colombia would lose a net amount of $63 million, or about 0.06% of GDP. In the longer term, however, Colombia would gain $550 million each year, or about a 0.5% permanent increase to GDP.[49]

Market Access for U.S. Exporters

Proponents of the agreement contend that it will improve market access for U.S. exporters. Much of the U.S. business community supports the FTA. They view it as an opportunity for U.S. businesses and for increasing exports of U.S. products, especially in agriculture. The National Pork Producers Council, for example, argues that a trade agreement will provide significant new

---

[46] IIE, August 2006, pp. 88-89.

[47] USITC Publication 3896, p. xv.

[48] Ibid, pp. xvi-xvii.

[49] IIE, August, 2006.

export opportunities for U.S. pork producers.[50] The business community often states that an FTA with Colombia will "level the playing field" with Colombia by providing U.S. producers of goods and services the same access to the Colombian market that Colombian businesses currently have in the U.S. market. They also believe that a trade agreement would give U.S. businesses a competitive edge in Colombia over other foreign-owned businesses.

U.S. exporters are concerned that they are losing market share in the Colombian market as a result of passage of free trade agreements that Colombia has negotiated with other countries. Some U.S. exporters are especially concerned about the Colombia-Canada free trade agreement that recently entered into force. U.S. wheat producers estimate that the falling U.S. share of the Colombian wheat import market will decline even further as a result of the implementation of Colombia's FTA with Canada.[51]

Colombia's Free Trade Agreements with Other Countries

Numerous policymakers voiced concern about the United States losing market share of the Colombian market if Congress did not approve the U.S.-Colombia FTA. Over the past ten years, Colombia has been actively negotiating free trade agreements with other countries. Colombia has five FTAs with 12 countries in Latin America. In addition, the Colombia-Canada FTA entered into force on August 15, 2011. Colombia has signed FTAs with the European Union, and the EFTA (Iceland, Liechtenstein, Norway, and Switzerland). Colombia has also joined an effort to create a regional trade integration agreement with Chile, Mexico, and Peru by signing a declaration for this effort on April 28, 2011.

The United States is Colombia's leading trading partner and the leading supplier of Colombia's imports, but its market share has been declining since 2000. Between 2000 and 2010, the share of Colombia's imports supplied from the United States declined from 34% to 26%. In agriculture goods, Argentina replaced the United States as the leading supplier of Colombia's agriculture imports in 2010, likely due to a preferential trade arrangement with the region. In 2000, the United States supplied 31% of Colombian imports of agricultural products, while Argentina supplied only 5%. By 2010, Argentina's share had risen to 26% while the United States' share had declined to 13%. Policymakers are concerned that the U.S. market share of Colombian imports will fall even further once the Colombia-Canada FTA enters into force.

Issues Related to Labor

Numerous U.S. labor groups oppose the pending free trade agreement with Colombia. They maintain that Colombia's labor movement is under attack through violence, intimidation, and harassment, as well as legal channels. The American Federation of Labor and Congress of Industrial Organizations (AFL-CIO), which is strongly opposed to the agreement, contends that Colombian labor union members face daily legal challenges to their rights to organize and bargain collectively and that these challenges threaten the existence of the Colombian labor movement. While the AFL-CIO acknowledges that Colombia has made progress in protecting union members, it continues to have concerns regarding the government's commitment to protect

---

[50] National Pork Producers Council, *NPCC Applauds President for Sending Trade Deal to Congress,* April 7, 2008.

[51] National Association of Wheat Growers, *Fact Sheet: U.S.-Colombia Free Trade Agreement,* April 2011.

fundamental worker rights.[52] The AFL-CIO remains opposed to the FTA even after the Action Plan negotiated by the Obama Administration and the Colombian government was announced on April 6, 2011.[53] On April 3, 2012, in view of President Obama's upcoming trip to Cartagena, Colombia for the Summit of the Americas, AFL-CIO President Richard Trumka wrote a letter to the President in which he said that Colombia was failing to fully comply with its commitments under the Action Plan. He stated that the Colombian government had failed to halt the "violent repression of labor and other human rights activists" and that it was "premature to declare the Labor Action Plan a success." He warned that moving too quickly toward implementation of the FTA could jeopardize future improvements for Colombian workers and harm workers of both countries.[54]

The position of Colombian labor unions on the U.S.-Colombia FTA is mixed, with some unions in favor of the agreement and others opposed. In May 2007, 17 Colombian unionists representing the textiles, flower, mining, and other Colombian industries visited the U.S. Congress to speak out in favor of the agreement. They represented the General Labor Confederation of Colombia (CGT), which has acknowledged progress in protecting worker rights by the Colombian government. Union members in support of an FTA argue that an FTA would provide jobs in the coffee, flower, textiles, and other industries in Colombia. They contend that the Uribe Administration made much progress in protecting worker rights and that the Santos Administration is making these positive changes "more concrete." Some CGT representatives do not believe that union workers are being targeted for their labor activities and believe that the violence is due to the ongoing conflict in Colombia caused by guerillas and paramilitaries.[55]

Other Colombian union representatives, however, many of whom are government employees, have spoken out against the agreement. They argue that an FTA would interfere with the Colombian government's right to govern the country, and that it would have a negative effect on Colombia's agriculture sector and the economy in general.[56] A major labor confederation in Colombia, the Central Union of Workers (CUT) is strongly opposed to the FTA with the United States and argues that an FTA with the United States would not be effective in protecting worker rights in Colombia because the labor chapter in the agreement does not go far enough to protect worker rights. The CUT also contends that the Action Plan Related to Labor Rights would not be effective in ending the impunity of crimes against unionists in Colombia. According to a CUT representative, the main problem in Colombia is the high levels of impunity and the lack of justice in the legal system.[57]

In the ILO's 2010 *Report of the Committee of Experts on the Application of Conventions and Recommendations* (CEACR), the ILO expressed satisfaction regarding the measures the Colombian government had taken in improving protection of freedom of association and collective bargaining.[58] The 2010 ILO report on the application of labor standards removed

---

[52] *Colombia Reports,* "Colombia too far behind on labor and human rights: U.S. union," March 21, 2010.

[53] AFL-CIO Now Blog, *AFL-CIO Remains Opposed to Colombia Trade Deal,* April 7, 2011.

[54] Richard L. Trumka, American Federation of Labor and Congress of Industrial Organizations, letter to President Barack Obama, April 3, 2012.

[55] In-person interview with representatives of the General Labor Confederation (CGT) of Colombia on June 2, 2011.

[56] Central Union of Workers of Colombia (CUT), *Rechazamos el TLC Por Ello, Desautorizamos toda Opinión Sindical que Contrarie la Postura Institucional,* April 12, 2007. CUT, *TLC: Todos Limosnearemos Comida,* April 2008.

[57] In-person interview with CUT representatives on June 1, 2011.

[58] ILO, *2010 Report of the Committee of Experts on the Application of Conventions and Recommendations,* February (continued...)

Colombia from the 25 countries it examined for failure to comply with international labor standards. However, the report noted that Colombia was taken off the list after a lengthy debate and that it had been taken off the list to break a gridlock in that particular year.[59]

In response to U.S. concerns regarding worker rights in Colombia, the Embassy of Colombia in the United States has been reporting the progress that Colombia has made since 2001 in strengthening the rights, benefits, and security of unions in Colombia. According to progress reports issued by the embassy, government reforms in Colombia since 2002 have helped protect Colombian worker rights to form unions, bargain collectively, and strike. These include enhanced efforts to open dialogue with union members, including meetings with the president and vice president of Colombia.[60] A September 2011 report issued by the embassy provides data indicating that homicides dropped by 45% since 2000 and that homicides of union members decreased 81% during the same period. Another report states that a protection program aimed at vulnerable groups, including union members, and the creation of the special unit at the Prosecutor General's Office have led to an 86% reduction in the level of homicides of union members. Regarding allegations that Colombia is the world's most dangerous country for union members, the Colombian government responds that because other countries do not track this data, the data cannot be compared with different countries. The government argues that union membership in certain professions in Colombia is almost universal, including teachers and judicial branch employees, and that when someone in these professions is murdered, it is often a union member. The government believes that many of victims of violence happen to be union members, but that does not necessarily mean that they were targeted because of their union activities.[61]

Issues Related to Colombia's Labor Cooperatives

Many Members of Congress have expressed concerns about labor cooperatives in Colombia. Colombian cooperatives are work arrangements mostly found in the sugar cane, palm oil, flower, mining, and port industries. Critics of the programs contend that this type of work arrangement leads to a lack of protection of worker rights, wages below the minimum wage, and lower health and pension benefits.[62] The Colombian government established these work arrangements to help generate employment, but it later recognized these pacts could lead to an erosion of worker rights. Subsequently, it has undertaken a series of reforms since 2004. The most recent law was passed by Colombia's Congress on December 12, 2010. Article 63 of *Ley 1429*, a law for formalizing the labor force and generating employment, has new and stronger measures to help ensure that worker rights are not being violated and to impose sanctions on businesses that are violating Colombian laws.[63] The major changes in this law are increased sanctions on companies for violations of the law from about $25,000 to $1.5 million; accountability for

---

(...continued)

2010, at http://www.ilo.org/ilolex/gbe/ceacr2010 htm.

[59] ILO, *Conference Committee on the Application of Standards: Extracts from the Record of Proceedings (ILC 2010)*, at http://www.ilo.org/global.

[60] Embassy of Colombia, Washington, D.C., *Colombia: A Progress Report: Strengthening the Rights, Benefits, and Security of Unions*, October 2007.

[61] Embassy of Colombia, Washington, D.C., *Answers to Frequent Allegations about Colombia and Labor Violence*, September 2011.

[62] Mark Gruenberg, "Colombian labor leader seeks trade pact delay," *People's World*, January 21, 2011.

[63] In-person interview with Colombian Embassy staff in Washington, D.C. and the Vice Minister of Labor from the Colombian government on March 10, 2011.

inspectors if they do not enforce the law; and enhanced bargaining rights for workers belonging to a cooperative. The law was to have a transition period and not enter into effect until July 2013. However, in an agreement with the United States under the Action Plan Related to Labor Rights, the Colombian government agreed to accelerate implementation of the law to June 2011.[64]

Critics of the cooperative work arrangements contend that the arrangements lead to worker oppression, prevent workers from joining unions, and result in a denial of basic benefits; critics also contend that certain marginalized groups, especially the Afro-Colombian population, are particularly vulnerable to unfair treatment. Colombian labor representatives urged Congress to delay passage of the FTA until Colombia improved its labor laws.[65]

According to the Colombian government, cooperatives are required to provide health benefits, worker rights protections, and pension benefits. However, there have been many cases of non-compliance. Documents obtained from the Colombian government show that, between 2007 and January 2011, inspectors made 4,787 visits to work areas, conducted 4,052 investigations, and imposed sanctions 816 times. The documents also show that the number of workers participating in cooperatives decreased from 2 million in 2007 to 600,000 in 2010, and that the number of cooperatives decreased from 12,317 to 4,555 between 2007 and 2010.[66]

Violence Issues

Numerous Members of Congress oppose the FTA with Colombia because of concerns about violence in Colombia against labor union members and other human rights defenders. Policymakers who have voiced opposition to the agreement generally are concerned about the impunity issue in Colombia, the lack of investigations and prosecutions, and the role of the paramilitary. Some Members argued that the high rate of violence in Colombia made it an "unfit free trade agreement partner for the United States."[67] The Obama Administration also expressed concerns about the level of violence in Colombia and negotiated the "Action Plan Related to Labor Rights" discussed earlier in this report.

Republican and some Democratic supporters of the FTA take issue with some charges against the Colombian government and contend that Colombia has made significant progress in recent years to curb the violence. Certain Members stated that Colombia is a crucial ally of the United States in Latin America and that if the FTA with Colombia was not passed, it would have led to further problems in the region. In a report issued by USTR, a number of quotes by Members of Congress in support of a trade agreement with Colombia were compiled. They were generally quoted as saying that the agreement had implications for the security interests of the United States in Colombia and that Colombia had made significant progress in cutting down on the number of murders and other criminal activities.[68]

---

[64] The White House, Office of the Press Secretary, "Leveling the Playing Field: Labor Protections and the U.S.-Colombia Trade Promotion Agreement," April 6, 2011, available at http://www.whitehouse.gov/the-press-office/2011/04/06/fact-sheets-us-colombia-trade-agreement-and-action-plan.

[65] Mark Gruenberg, "Colombian labor leader seeks trade pact delay," *People's World,* January 21, 2011.

[66] Data obtain from an in-person interview with a Vice-Minister from the Colombian government's Ministerio de la Protección Social on March 10, 2011.

[67] BNA, *International Trade Reporter,* "Five Democratic Lawmakers Blast Proposed Colombia FTA Due to Violence," June 14, 2007.

[68] Office of the United States Trade Representative, *Broad Support for U.S.-Colombia Free Trade Agreement: What* (continued...)

The Colombian government has responded to U.S. concerns and acknowledged that, while there continue to be killings in Colombia, the situation has improved significantly since the Uribe Administration. Government reports indicate that over 50,000 guerrilla members were demobilized as a result of the government's recovery of control over territory and the implementation of a peace process with paramilitary groups. In addition, Colombian government reports state that confessions obtained from former paramilitaries and guerillas have provided important information in the investigation of past violence, including that against union members.[69] Government data indicate that assassinations of labor union activists and teachers decreased by 86% between 2002 and 2009, from 196 in 2002 to 28 in 2009. In 2010, however, this number increased to 37. Total homicides in Colombia decreased from 28,837 in 2002 to 15,459 in 2010 (a 46% decrease).[70] Homicides of labor union members account for a small percentage of total homicides in Colombia: 0.2% of total homicides in 2010.

Author Contact Information

M. Angeles Villarreal
Specialist in International Trade and Finance
avillarreal@crs.loc.gov, 7-0321

(...continued)

They're Saying, March 2008.

[69] Embassy of Colombia, *Ensuring Justice and Protecting Labor and Human Rights in Colombia,* 2010.

[70] Embassy of Colombia, *Answers to Frequent Allegations about Colombia and Labor Violence,* September 2011. Data on homicides in Colombia is from Colombia's Ministry of Defense and the Ministry of Social Protection.

---

www.ingramcontent.com/pod-product-compliance
Lightning Source LLC
Chambersburg PA
CBHW081243170526
45165CB00009B/3172

* 9 7 8 1 4 8 2 0 7 5 9 7 7 *